CARRIE PEOPLES' READING SYSTEM

FROM BABBLE TO READING

by
Carrie Peoples

edited by
Danielle Yette

DORRANCE
PUBLISHING CO
EST. 1920
PITTSBURGH, PENNSYLVANIA 15238

Dorrance Publishing Co
585 Alpha Drive
Suite 103
Pittsburgh, PA 15238
Visit our website at www.dorrancebookstore.com

ISBN: 978-1-6480-4591-2
eISBN: 978-1-6480-4615-5

This book is dedicated to

Dr. John M. Jenkins (RIP) and his wife Diane Avis Jenkins who were responsible for guiding me toward a career as a Professional Educator, into Higher Education and graduation from Federal City College, now named University of the District of Columbia.

CARRIE PEOPLES' READING SYSTEM

FROM BABBLE TO READING

INTRODUCTION

INFORMATION IS THE MOST VALUABLE COMMODITY ON EARTH. WE BUY AND SELL MORE INFORMATION THAN ANYTHING.

Children learn most of what they need in life between birth and five years old. They build learning processes and knowledge on that foundation with reiteration through our education processes. In order to ensure children have the base necessary it is imperative they receive the fundamental tools to process information prior to reaching school age.

Taking time to teach your child, first, personalizes the learning process. This shared experience will give you and your youngster the opportunity to bond through learning this foundation of our communication and educational process. As you implement this reading system you, your child and your family will develop new areas of independence as well as dependence for the purpose of knowledge building. Families interacting within this realm is a warm and beautiful experience for all. Confidence toward learning will develop and grow naturally. Success comes with a child's understanding and acceptance that strengthening her human nature and purpose in life is constant. We must consciously and continuously build positive KNOWLEDGE, SKILLS, ABILITIES AND ATTITUDES to compete in our rapidly changing society.

Think, corporations invest millions of dollars on retraining adult workers to learn communication skills: listening, writing, reading, and data usage. By developing these skills early, you are ensuring that children are ready with essential skills to be at the forefront for opportunities awaiting them in their futures.

1. Work with each child for about twenty to thirty minutes every day.

By taking the lead and the time to follow this process, your children will comprehend the importance of reading. Use this reading system daily so it will become an enjoyable routine that is looked forward to. This parent-child activity has many positives while learning language, encouraging and enabling verbal and cognitive growth.

2. Ask each child to tell you a story.

You are to use the child's personal storytelling with this systematic approach to teach reading. Keep in mind, children have millions of words, ideas, pictures in their minds. As you delve into these procedures, you will discover at 2 and 3 years old, children's cognitive development is amazingly complex, although complete development continues into adulthood. At an early age, you will learn the rapid rate at which your child's intelligence is expanding. Trust this, your child will love this positive interaction and so will you. Encourage your child to practice leadership skills by selecting the topic. Time your activities to no more than 30 minutes each day. Allow your child to set the timer, that also is a learned skill. Lead, never push your thoughts into the minds of children and please do not rush them through these procedures. Be a kind, gentle listener.

3. You will record them as they speak.

You will need a device to record the story each child tells you. This can be a tape recorder, an application on a cellular phone or any other device that will reach the end result.

Explain and demonstrate what it means to be recorded, so he is comfortable. Allow him to practice speaking into the instrument then, play it back as you watch his entire being light up while he listens to his story. Never interrupt him, simply capture his personal information; accept his thoughts.

 Decide if you will transcribe in handwriting or if you will type. Typing will clearly show the symbols that we use to make what we call words.

4. You will write down what they say exactly as they say it with no corrections.

While your child is speaking DO NOT CORRECT her. Transcribe each word exactly as she says it in order to be completely owned by her. This will be an exact depiction of her thoughts. This will assist her in understanding her words and thoughts in the future. It will also lead to an accurate depiction of where she began the reading process.

5. One page per day

The story from each child should amount to one page per day. That is all that is needed for this process. The number of words from each child and day may vary. This process should be enjoyable.

6. Each day, have your child read the story told the previous day.

To begin each portion of time spent together for reading, have the child read the story they told the previous day. Stories may change and may not match what is on the page at all. This will get more precise as time goes on. Children's procedural understanding will strengthen with practice.

7. At the end of each week, have the child read the five stories told to you.

At the end of each week, have your child dictate each story told to you. They may still add or exclude information and that is alright. Your child is beginning an editing process to allow recognition of accuracies and errors. By having produced and read their own stories throughout the week they will easily take ownership and recall details. Give praises for a job well done!

8. When you get about twenty to thirty stories, begin to make their "books" with cardboard and nice material or paper as a cover. Soon they will have many "books".

Have the materials necessary for the creation of your child's "books": nice paper with lines, cardboard, material (cloth or durable designed paper), glue or paste, pencils or markers.

Creating "books" is a way for children to nurture their stories and feel ownership that each one is important. They are now building a personal knowledge base of thoughts and feelings shared as the authors of their very own books. As crafting stories becomes a priority, you will discover there is no end to her stories. The routine of authoring books will become second nature. At some point in this process, you will refer to his/her books as a personal collection and eventually "(Your Child's Name Here)'s Library".

Now you are ready to introduce organization skill building. Use words you want your child to grasp as you organize her books by date. Surprisingly, you are teaching procedures, in early childhood, she will grow up to remember and use for life. Ownership is very important in linking processes of thoughts, knowledge, feelings, nurturing, caring. Recognizing and using words and phrases relative to the crafting of stories will indeed enrich and build a dynamic thinker. As you and your child organize stories by date, you and she will be able to monitor her progress.

9. Allow them to listen to their recorded stories anytime they want.

You are boosting listening and processing of information skills as you allow children to hear themselves speak. After a while, you will also find them trying to follow along in their "books". This is an amazing learning process at this point. Children who gain abilities to edit their own thinking, to envision how they want others to perceive their work is clearly a move toward higher thinking skills, detail adjustments, courageous planning of next moves.

10. Be patient with them, and they will soon be reading everything just as they read their stories!

Patience please, with new thoughts there will be corrections. As children's abilities to process information become more efficient and with realization of new knowledge, with the occurrence of more precise characterization, you will notice the linking of learning processes and growth in your youngster's desire for bigger ideas and more elaborate displays of art from his thoughts with an audience in mind. Think of that, at an early age, the self is concerned with another's thoughts. You both will feel those amazing accomplishments. Keep in mind, brain development continues through childhood, adolescence, on through young adulthood.

Teach your child that every symbol we use is simply a combination of circles, lines and dots. For example— 3 (two half circles); 5 (two lines and a half circle); M (four lines positioned to make what we call an M). Have them practice writing combinations of circles, lines and dots. They will soon learn how symbols need to be placed in order to make words.

Use index cards or paper and a pencil, marker or computer to make signs for everything in your living environment, (CHAIR, REFRIGERATOR, COUNTER, TOILET, BED...). Teach them that there is nothing complicated about reading and writing; they must simply learn the systems for those skills and practice them regularly. Also, teach them early that everything we do in our society is based on a system.

11. Connect words to pictures.

Most children are able to draw before they read and write. Give them a sheet of paper to draw about the stories they tell you. These can be included in their "books". As your child matures mentally the pictures will begin to match the words on the pages. Then you not only have an author, but an illustrator, as well.

12. Save your money for college.

Reading is the foundation of educational success. Setting this groundwork provides your child the gift of reading comprehension based on his own thoughts. Instilling this art of composition will prepare your child for unlimited future accomplishments.

Begin a savings account for your child's education. You have begun the process that will make the difference for the rest of your child's life!

Tried and True

I can remember Carrie's reading system, at 6 years of age, I spoke of how I love strawberries. I remember going into details about eating them. Carrie used a voice recorder to tape me, then she wrote out by hand what was recorded in my own words. I read it back and continued to add more. I believe that was my beginning to desire storytelling. I was basically illiterate at the time and having trouble in school, but her technique helped me to master my reading skills. I will be forever grateful to Carrie Peoples.

–Yaffa Lawson

I am excited to see this work in print. While visiting Carrie in 2012 just after the birth of my great grandson, Ty, she informed me of a program of hers that could have him reading before age 3. She printed the plan and gave it to me. As soon as Ty began to use words I put the program into action. By age 3 he amazed my family with the ability to read and recite the contents of THE BOOKS OF THE OLD TESTAMENT.

-Jean Ray

CPSIA information can be obtained
at www.ICGtesting.com
Printed in the USA
BVHW012116011022
648364BV00003B/11

9 781648 045912